LAND AND WATER

How Geography Affects Our Community

BY LISA ORAM

Editorial Offices: Glenview, Illinois • Parsippany, New Jersey • New York, New York

Sales Offices: Needham, Massachusetts • Duluth, Georgia • Glenview, Illinois
Coppell, Texas • Sacramento, California • Mesa, Arizona

Different Kinds of Geography

If you live near an ocean, you can spend time swimming and playing in the water. Someone you know might earn money by fishing or driving a tugboat. In a coastal **community**, people's way of life is connected to the ocean.

If you live in a desert, your daily life is probably very different. You might eat toast with jam made from the fruit of a Saguaro cactus. Your family might like to hike on cliffs and in canyons.

People live in many different places, and each **location** affects the communities that are found in these places.

Cactuses grow in the deserts.

Each different environment has benefits and challenges for the people who live there. To survive in different surroundings, people adapt, or adjust to them.

In some cases people must adapt to the land. In cold climates, for example, you cannot change the weather but you can learn how to keep warm. Sometimes,

In cold climates people need warm clothing.

people change the land to fit their needs. In the mountains people have made tunnels and roads in the mountains to make travel easier.

Living near Water

When you look at a globe, you will see that most of Earth's surface is covered with water. Bodies of water cover almost three-fourths of Earth. Most of that water is the ocean.

Oceans are huge bodies of salt water that separate large areas of land. There are four oceans on Earth. The Pacific Ocean is the largest, and it borders the western United States. The Atlantic Ocean borders the eastern United States. The Indian Ocean contains many islands. The Arctic Ocean has parts that are frozen all year long.

Many of the world's largest cities are located on ocean coasts. In the United States there are larger **populations** on the coasts than in between.

The fishing and shipping industries provide jobs for people who live in coastal cities.

Communities are often located near rivers. As water from rain and melting snow moves from high places like mountains to lower places like oceans or lakes, a system of rivers and streams is formed.

Rivers are also important for **transportation**. Before there were many roads, rivers were an important way to travel across land. After, towns were built near them and away from rivers. Populations grew in areas far from rivers. Today, the Mississippi River is a waterway for cargo boats.

People enjoy sporting activities at many lakes.

Lakes are bodies of water surrounded on all sides by land. Many lakes began thousands of years ago when large sheets of ice called glaciers moved slowly across Earth. These glaciers carved holes that filled with water from rain or melting ice.

Many people enjoy living around lakes because of their natural beauty and the opportunities they provide for sporting activities. In lake communities, people may enjoy boating, fishing, and swimming. Lake areas often get a lot of snow, so they are also good for skiing and sledding.

Lake areas attract a lot of visitors. Tourism can be big business in lake communities.

Some people live on islands. Islands are pieces of land that are surrounded on all sides by water. Islands are found in oceans.

Some islands are often small and have less than one hundred residents. Some islands are home to an entire country. The interior land on many islands is mountainous. This means the population may be the greatest on the outer edges of the island.

Travel between islands and the mainland affects life on the island. People can drive over bridges or through tunnels to get to and from some islands. Other islands, however, can only be reached by plane, boat, or ship.

People who live on islands must plan carefully if they depend on supplies from somewhere else. When there is bad weather, people on islands may be unable to get supplies they need.

Bridges to an island may be safer to travel on than boats and planes during bad weather.

There are many benefits to living near water, but communities must be careful not to harm Earth's water environments.

In coastal areas, huge cities with millions of people can strain the area's natural resources. Sandy shorelines can be worn away. Ocean water can become polluted. The fish and shellfish that feed many people can be taken out of the ocean faster than they can be replaced.

Only three percent of Earth's water supply is the fresh water that people drink. Water pollution is a threat to this water.

People must protect the water, but they must also protect themselves from dangerous weather that sometimes comes to coastal communities.

Hurricanes with heavy rains can cause floods that damage homes and buildings. In very rainy seasons rivers can overflow. People who live near water must know how to be safe.

Living in a Desert

Deserts are dry places that receive less than ten inches of rain per year. Even though water is so important to life, people have lived in deserts since ancient times.

Desert land can be sandy or rocky. There may be large flat areas as well as hills in desert areas. Animals and plants that live and grow in the desert have adapted to having little water.

Desert weather can be extreme. The days are very hot, and the nights are very cold. There are sandstorms, high winds, and blowing sand. When it rains, it can be sudden and often heavy, so there can be floods.

A small area within a desert with a good water source and many green plants is called an oasis. Some people who live in the desert may live near an oasis and move from place to place as the water supply changes. Their homes are tents that are light and easy to pack and carry.

In modern desert homes there may be air conditioning. People try to stay indoors during the hottest parts of the day.

Desert clothing also must be light to keep a person's body cool and protected from the sun. It is important to wear a hat and sunblock!

Some deserts are cold instead of hot. The continent of Antarctica is a desert. Even though there is lots of ice and snow, it hardly ever rains or snows there.

Living near Mountains

Mountains are tall, natural landforms that rise into peaks, or tops. Much of the land on mountains is covered by forests. The tallest mountains have snow on their peaks. As the temperature changes, the snow from high up on a mountain melts and runs down the mountain into streams and rivers where it provides water for people. In this way, mountains are one of Earth's most valuable resources.

For early explorers getting over or around mountains was very difficult. Today, there are roads over some mountains and tunnels through some mountains.

There are many countries, however, where it is still hard to move around in the mountains. In these areas getting supplies from place to place can be difficult. Most of the land is not good for farming, so survival still can be challenging for people living in some mountain areas.

In the valleys growing some food is possible. There also may be urban centers on the edges of mountain areas where living is easier.

Many people enjoy taking vacations in mountain areas.

Sharing the Land

All communities share their surroundings with plants and animals. There are some flowers that grow only in the mountains and others that grow only in the desert. Camels can live in the desert because they can survive with little water. Each environment influences the plants and animals that live there.

Every community is special, and all communities create a **culture** with customs and traditions related to the environment around them. Transportation, food, and clothes are all affected by where people live.

Visiting communities around the world can be both exciting and interesting. If you want to try skiing, you can go to the mountains. If you want to explore the desert, you can visit Arizona. If you have never played in the ocean waves, you might want to give it a try.

Each kind of landscape—deserts, mountains, lakes, rivers, and oceans—all offer important resources to communities. Earth is one place we all need to take care of and share.

Glossary

community a place where people live, work, and have fun together

culture the arts, beliefs, behavior, and ideas of a group of people

location where something can be found

population the number of people in an area

transportation a way of carrying things or people from place to place

Write to It!

You have read about many kinds of communities with different geographical features. Which type of community would you most like to live in? Why? Write one paragraph about your ideas.

Write your paragraph on another sheet of paper.

Photographs

Every effort has been made to secure permission and provide appropriate credit for photographic material. The publisher deeply regrets any omission and pledges to correct errors called to its attention in subsequent editions.

Unless otherwise acknowledged, all photographs are the property of Scott Foresman, a division of Pearson Education.

Photo locators denoted as follows: Top (T), Center (C), Bottom (B), Left (L), Right (R), Background (Bkgd)

Opener: (T) ©Getty Images, (C) ©Getty Images, (B) ©Getty Images
2 ©Royalty-Free/Corbis, (Bkgd T, B) ©Digital Vision, (Bkgd L, R) ©Getty Images
3 ©Ronnie Kaufman/Corbis
5 ©Getty Images
6 ©AP/Wide World Photos
7 ©Bob Krist/Corbis
9 ©James Marshall/Corbis
10 ©Frans Lemmens/Getty Images
13 ©Royalty-Free/Corbis
15 ©Getty Images

Fascinating Facts

- The Nile River in Egypt is the world's longest river, but the Amazon River in Brazil moves the most water.

- The world's largest freshwater lake is Lake Baikal in Russia.

- The highest temperature ever recorded in the world is 136°F (58°C) in the Sahara.

Genre	Comprehension Skill	Text Features
Nonfiction	Main Idea and Details	• Glossary • Headings • Captions

Scott Foresman Social Studies

PEARSON

Scott
Foresman

scottforesman.com

ISBN 0-328-14824-5

90000

9 780328 148240

Many Leaves

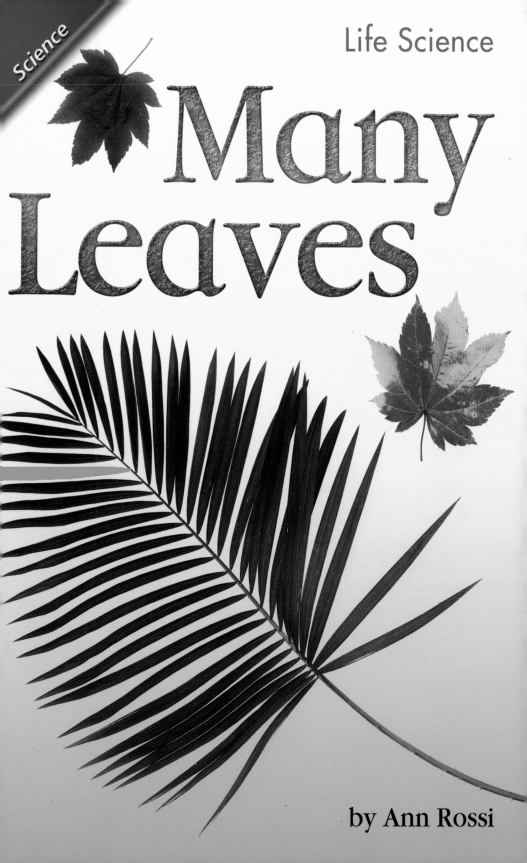

by Ann Rossi

Vocabulary	Extended Vocabulary
antennae	compound
camouflage	conifer
flower	evergreen
leaf	float
root	simple
stem	spines

Picture Credits

Every effort has been made to secure permission and provide appropriate credit for photographic material.
The publisher deeply regrets any omission and pledges to correct errors called to its attention in subsequent editions.

Photo locators denoted as follows: Top (T), Center (C), Bottom (B), Left (L), Right (R), Background (Bkgd).

8 (BR) ©Stephen Haywood/DK Images; 12 (BL) Peter Oxford/Nature Picture Library.

Unless otherwise acknowledged, all photographs are the copyright © of Dorling Kindersley, a division of Pearson.

ISBN: 0-328-13741-3

Copyright © Pearson Education, Inc. All Rights Reserved. Printed in the United States of America.
This publication is protected by Copyright, and permission should be obtained from the publisher prior to any
prohibited reproduction, storage in a retrieval system, or transmission in any form by any means, electronic,
mechanical, photocopying, recording, or likewise. For information regarding permission(s), write to
Permissions Department, Scott Foresman, 1900 East Lake Avenue, Glenview, Illinois 60025.

7 8 9 10 V010 13 12 11 10 09 08 07 06